T0115408

Mark Twain on Common Sense

Mark Twain on Common Sense

Timeless Advice and Words of
Wisdom from
America's Most-Revered
Humorist

Mark Twain

Skyhorse Publishing

Copyright © 2014 Skyhorse Publishing, Inc.

All rights reserved. No part of this book may be reproduced in any manner without the express written consent of the publisher, except in the case of brief excerpts in critical reviews or articles. All inquiries should be addressed to Skyhorse Publishing, 307 West 36th Street, 11th Floor, New York, NY 10018.

Skyhorse Publishing books may be purchased in bulk at special discounts for sales promotion, corporate gifts, fund-raising, or educational purposes. Special editions can also be created to specifications. For details, contact the Special Sales Department, Skyhorse Publishing, 307 West 36th Street, 11th Floor, New York, NY 10018 or info@skyhorsepublishing.com.

Skyhorse® and Skyhorse Publishing® are registered trademarks of Skyhorse Publishing, Inc.®, a Delaware corporation.

Visit our website at www.skyhorsepublishing.com.

10 9 8 7

Library of Congress Cataloging-in-Publication Data is available on file.

Cover design by Jane Sheppard
Cover photo credit Thinkstock

Print ISBN: 978-1-62873-799-8
Ebook ISBN: 978-1-62914-078-0

Printed in the United States of America

CONTENTS

Persons attempting to find a motive in this narration will be prosecuted; persons attempting to find a moral in it will be banished; persons attempting to find a plot in it will be shot.

By Order of the Author.

YOUTH AND OLD AGE

Always do right. This will gratify some people and astonish the rest.

The elastic heart of youth cannot be compressed into one constrained shape long at a time.

Adam and Eve had many advantages but the principal one was, that they escaped teething.

For the majority of us, the past is a regret, the future an experiment.

When I was a boy of fourteen, my father was so ignorant I could hardly stand to have the old man around. But when I was twenty-one, I was astonished at how much he had learned in seven years.

Genius has no youth, but starts with the ripeness of age and old experience.

I am an old man and have known a great many troubles, but most of them never happened.

There is but one solitary thing about the past worth remembering and that is the fact that it is past—and can't be restored.

Twenty years from now you will be more disappointed by the things you didn't do than by the ones you did do.

At fifty a man can be an ass without being an optimist, but not an optimist without being an ass.

The past may not repeat itself, but it sure does rhyme.

What is human life? The first third is a good time; the rest is remembering it.

Wrinkles should merely indicate where smiles have been.

The most interesting information comes from children, for they tell all they know and then stop.

Life would be infinitely happier if we could only be born at the age of eighty and gradually approach eighteen.

I was young and foolish then; now I am old and foolish.

The man who is a pessimist before forty-eight knows too much; if he is an optimist after it he knows too little.

Nothing that grieves us can be called little; by the eternal laws of proportion a child's loss of a doll and a king's loss of a crown are events of the same size.

He had double chins all the way down to his stomach.

When I was younger I could remember everything, whether it happened or not.

Whatever a man's age, he can reduce it by putting a bright-colored flower in his button-hole.

All say, how hard it is to have to die—a strange complaint to come from the mouths of people who have had to live.

Frankness is a jewel only the young can afford.

When your friends begin to flatter you on how young you look, it's a sure sign you're getting old.

The older we grow the greater becomes our wonder at how much ignorance one can contain without bursting one's clothes.

Get a bicycle. You will not regret it. If you live.

There comes a time in every rightly constructed boy's life that he has a raging desire to go somewhere and dig for hidden treasure.

No real estate is permanently valuable but the grave.

There is no sadder sight than a young pessimist.

Now and then we had a hope that if we lived and were good, God would permit us to be pirates.

It's well enough for old folks to rise early, because they have done so many mean things all their lives they can't sleep anyhow.

A baby is an inestimable blessing and bother.

Keep away from small people who try to belittle your ambition. Small people always do that, but the really great make you feel that you, too, can become great.

Often, the less there is to justify a traditional custom, the harder it is to get rid of it.

The only way to keep your health is to eat what you don't want, drink what you don't like, and do what you'd rather not.

It isn't so astonishing the number of things that I can remember, as the number of things that I can remember that aren't so.

We have not all had the good fortune to be ladies. We have not all been generals, or poets, or statesmen; but when the toast works down to the babies, we stand on common ground.

EDUCATION

You shouldn't try to teach a pig to sing. You waste your time and it annoys the pig.

Education consists mainly in what we have unlearned.

What's the use you learning to do right, when it's troublesome to do right and ain't no trouble to do wrong, and the wages is just the same?

Never learn to do anything. If you don't learn, you will always find someone else to do it for you.

The more you explain it, the more I don't understand it.

For all the talk you hear about knowledge being such a wonderful thing, instinct is worth forty of it for real unerringness.

A man never reaches that dizzy height of wisdom that he can no longer be led by the nose.

Everything has its limit—iron ore cannot be educated into gold.

Soap and education are not as sudden as a massacre, but they are more deadly in the long run.

Four years at West Point and plenty of books and schooling will learn a man a great deal. It won't learn him the river.

Don't go around thinking the world owes you a living. The world owes you nothing. It was here first.

Troubles are only mental; it is the mind that manufactures them, and the mind can gorge them, banish them, abolish them.

Life does not consist mainly, or even largely, of facts and happenings. It consists mainly of the storm of thought that is forever flowing through one's head.

Training is everything. The peach was once the bitter almond; cauliflower is nothing but cabbage with a college education.

Use the right word and not its second cousin.

Don't part with your illusions. When they are gone you may still exist, but you have ceased to live.

Education is the path from cocky ignorance to miserable uncertainty.

Intellectual work is misnamed; it is pleasure, a dissipation, and its own highest reward.

You may have noticed that the less I know about a subject the more confidence I have, and the more new light I throw on it.

You can't depend on your judgment when your imagination is out of focus.

Cast iron rules will not answer. What is one man's colon is another man's comma.

When I was a boy on the Mississippi River there was a proposition in a township there to discontinue public schools because they were too expensive. An old farmer spoke up and said that if they stopped building schools they would not save anything, because every time a school was closed a jail had to be built.

It is nobler to be good, and it is nobler still to teach others to be good—and less trouble!

Get the facts first. You can distort them later.

Poetry, like chastity, can be taken too far.

One learns through the heart, not the eyes or the intellect.

I don't give a damn for a man that can only spell a word one way.

A cat is more intelligent than people believe, and can be taught any crime.

It ain't what you don't know that gets you into trouble. It's what you know for sure that just ain't so.

I never let my schooling interfere with my education.

The difference between the right word and the almost right word is the difference between lightning and a lightning bug.

Some people get an education without going to college; the rest get it after they get out.

(on reading a bad book) Once you put it down, you simply can't pick it up.

We all do no end of feeling, and we mistake it for thinking.

Do something everyday that you do not want to do.

Ideally a book would have no order to it, and the reader would have to discover his own.

Why shouldn't truth be stranger than fiction? Fiction, after all, has to make sense.

Scientists have odious manners, except when you prop up their theory—then you can borrow money off them.

The trouble with the world is not that people know too little, but that they know so many things that ain't so.

Inherited ideas are a curious thing, and interesting to observe and examine.

Ignorant people think it's the noise which fighting cats make that is aggravating, but it ain't so; it's the sickening grammar they use.

GOVERNMENT, POLITICS, LAW, AND WAR

By the etiquette of war, it is permitted to none below the rank of newspaper correspondent to dictate to the general in the field.

Citizenship is what makes a republic; monarchies can get along without it.

Conservatism is the blind and fear-filled worship of dead radicals.

We have a criminal jury system which is superior to any in the world; and it's efficiency is only marred by the difficulty of finding twelve men every day who don't know anything and can't read.

To lodge all power in one party and keep it there is to insure bad government and the sure and gradual of the public morals.

I asked Tom if countries always apologized when they had done wrong, and he says: 'Yes. The little ones does.'

God made the Idiot for practice, and then He made the School Board.

Noise proves nothing. Often a hen who has merely laid an egg cackles as if she laid an asteroid.

I think I can say, and say with pride, that we have some legislatures that bring higher prices than any in the world.

Whenever you find yourself on the side of the majority, it is time to pause and reflect.

Every citizen of the republic ought to consider himself an unofficial policeman, and keep unsalaried watch and ward over the laws and their execution.

We all live in the protection of certain cowardices which we call our principles.

The rule is perfect: in all matters of opinion our adversaries are insane.

There is no salvation for us but to adopt Civilization and lift ourselves down to its level.

The radical of one century is the conservative of the next. The radical invents the views. When he has worn them out, the conservative adopts them.

We have the best government money can buy.

The political morals of the United States are not merely food for laughter, they are an entire banquet.

A conspiracy is nothing but a secret agreement of a number of men for the pursuance of policies which they dare not admit in public.

The more I get to know lawyers, the more I'm in favor of hangin'.

Loyalty to the country always. Loyalty to the government when it deserves it.

I've come loaded with statistics, for I've noticed that a man can't prove anything without statistics.

Sometimes I wonder whether the world is being run by smart people who are putting us on or by imbeciles who really mean it.

A nation is only an individual multiplied.

A man's first duty is to his own conscience and honor; the party and country come second to that, and never first.

The way it is now, the asylums can hold all the sane people but if we tried to shut up the insane we should run out of building materials.

It is my custom to keep on talking until I get the audience cowed.

In statesmanship get the formalities right, never mind about the moralities.

Principles have no real force except when one is well fed.

Principles aren't of much account anyway, except at election time. After that you hang them up to let them season. There is nothing in the world like a persuasive speech to fuddle the mental apparatus and upset the convictions and debauch the emotions of an audience not practiced in the tricks and delusions of oratory.

I could probably be shown by facts and figure that there is no distinctly American criminal class except Congress.

Fleas can be taught nearly anything that a congressman can.

We adore titles and heredities in our hearts and ridicule them with our mouths.

What is the difference between a taxidermist and a tax collector? The taxidermist takes only your skin.

An inglorious peace is better than a dishonorable war.

Whiskey is carried into the committee room in demijohns and carried out in demagogues.

Going to law is losing a cow for the sake of a cat.

I have no race prejudice. I think I have no color prejudices or caste prejudices. Indeed, I know it. I can't stand society. All that I care to know is that a man is a human being—that is enough for me; he can't be any worse.

We like a man to come right out and say what he thinks—if we agree with him.

When a man is known to have no settled convictions of his own he can't convict other people.

Only kings, presidents, editors, and people with tapeworms have the right to use the editorial "we".

Only when a republic's life is in danger should a man uphold his government when it is wrong. There is no other time.

The principle of give and take is the principle of diplomacy—give one and take ten.

Whenever you find that you are on the side of the majority, it is time to reform.

War talk by men who have been in a war is always interesting; whereas moon talk by a poet who has not been on the moon is likely to be dull. Great enterprises usually promise vastly more than they perform.

One has ever seen a Republican mass meeting that was devoid of the perception of the ludicrous.

Suppose you were an idiot and suppose you were a member of Congress. But I repeat myself.

All war must be the killing of strangers against whom you feel no personal animosity; strangers whom, in other circumstances, you would help if you found them in trouble, and who would help you if you needed it.

We are discreet sheep; we wait to see how the drove is going, and then go with the drove.

There is no end to the laws, and no beginning to the execution of them.

Each man must for himself alone decide what is right and what is wrong, which course is patriotic and which isn't. You cannot shirk this and be a man. To decide against your conviction is to be an unqualified and inexcusable traitor, both to yourself and to your country. Let them label you as they may.

The conviction of the rich that the poor are happier is no more foolish than the conviction of the poor that the rich are.

A newspaper is not just for reporting the news as it is, but to make people mad enough to do something about it.

Only a government that is rich and safe can afford to be a democracy, for democracy is the most expensive and nefarious kind of government ever heard of on earth.

The innocent who could laugh with joy didn't dare to because they were sitting beside a guilty friend who didn't dare to.

LOVE

Comedy keeps the heart sweet.

When you fish for love, bait with your heart not your brain.

There are women who have an indefinable charm in their faces which makes them beautiful to their intimates, but a cold stranger who tried to reason the matter out and find this beauty would fail.

Sanity and happiness are an impossible combination.

Kindness is a language which the deaf can hear and the blind can see.

Women cannot receive even the most palpably judicious suggestion without arguing it, that is, married women.

Heroine: girl who is perfectly charming to live with, in a book.

Man will do many things to get himself loved; he will do all things to get himself envied.

When a man's dog turns against him it is time for his wife to pack her bag and go home to mama.

Chastity—you can carry it too far.

Any emotion, if it is sincere, is involuntary.

Love is a madness; if thwarted, it develops fast.

There is only one good sex. The female one.

A soiled baby, with a neglected nose, cannot be conscientiously regarded as a thing of beauty.

What would men be without women? Scarce, sir, mighty scarce.

The holy passion of friendship is so sweet and steady and loyal and enduring in nature that it will last through a whole lifetime, if not asked to lend money.

We are always too busy for our children; we never give them the time or interest they deserve. We lavish gifts upon them; but the most precious gift, our personal association, which means so much to them, we give grudgingly.

Let's make a special effort to stop communicating with each other, so we can have some conversation.

The best way to cheer yourself up is to try to cheer someone else up.

Everyone is a moon, and has a dark side which he never shows to anybody.

Familiarity breeds contempt, also children.

There is a lot to say in her favor, but the other is more interesting.

Both marriage and death ought to be welcome: the one promises happiness, doubtless the other assures it.

While the rest of the species is descended from apes, redheads are descended from cats.

Conscience takes up more room than all the rest of a person's insides.

Our opinions do not really blossom into fruition until we have expressed them to someone else.

To get the full value of joy you must have someone to divide it with.

Modesty died when clothes were born.

It takes your enemy and your friend, working together to hurt you to the heart; the one to slander you and the other to get the news to you.

HONESTY AND ITS OPPOSITE

Etiquette requires us to admire the human race.

Often, the surest way to convey misinformation is to tell the strict truth.

If you tell the truth you don't have to remember anything.

A lie can travel halfway around the world while the truth is still putting on its shoes.

When in doubt, tell the truth.

I never did a thing in all my life, virtuous or otherwise, that I didn't repent of within twenty-four hours.

We are always more anxious to be distinguished for a talent which we do not possess, than to be praised for the fifteen we do possess.

A man's private thought can never be a lie; what he thinks, is to him the truth, always.

It is easier to manufacture seven facts out of whole cloth than one emotion.

But that's always the way; it don't make no difference whether you do right or wrong, a person's conscience ain't got no sense, and just goes for him anyway ... It takes up more room than all the rest of a person's insides . . . "

It is not likely that any complete life has ever been lived which was not a failure in the secret judgment of the person that lived it.

Honesty is the best policy—when there is money in it.

You perceive I generalize with intrepidity from single instances.

George Washington, as a boy, was ignorant of the commonest accomplishments of youth. He could not even lie.

Familiarity breeds contempt. How accurate that is. The reason we hold truth in such respect is because we have so little opportunity to get familiar with it.

A man is never more truthful than when he acknowledges himself a liar.

The statue that advertises its modesty with a fig leaf really brings its modesty under suspicion.

Never tell a lie, except for practice.

I have a higher standard of principle than George Washington. He could not lie; I can but I won't.

Do not tell fish stories where the people know you; particularly, don't tell them where they know the fish.

I never could tell a lie that anyone would doubt, nor a truth that anyone would believe.

Prophecy is a good line of business, but it is full of risks.

I am not one of those who in expressing opinions confine themselves to facts.

No man is straightly honest to any but himself and God.

I have been cautioned to talk, but to be careful not to say anything. I do not consider this a difficult task.

My parents were neither very poor nor conspicuously honest.

No one is willing to acknowledge a fault in himself when a more agreeable motive can be found for the estrangement of his acquaintances.

There's one way to find out if a man is honest: ask him; if he says yes, you know he is crooked.

An author values a compliment even when it comes from a source of doubtful competency.

It is often the case that the man who can't tell a lie thinks he is the best judge of one.

There are people who think that honesty is always the best policy. This is a superstition; there are times when the appearance of it is worth six of it.

What a good thing Adam had. When he said a good thing he knew nobody had said it before. There are no grades of vanity, there are only grades of ability in concealing it.

A crowded police court docket is the surest of all signs that trade is brisk and money plenty.

It is no use to keep private information which you can't show off.

I like the truth sometimes, but I don't care enough to hanker after it.

The first of April is the day we remember what we are the other 364 days of the year.

Better a broken promise than none at all.

Never tell the truth to people who are not worthy of it.

Truth is tough. It will not break, like a bubble, at a touch; nay, you may kick it about all day, like a football, and it will be round and full at evening.

Is a person's public and private opinion the same? It is thought there have been instances.

Truth is mighty and will prevail. There is nothing wrong with this, except that it ain't so.

There are lies, damn lies and statistics.

In writing, I shall always confine myself strictly to the truth, except when it is attended with inconvenience.

We must put up with clothes as they have their reason for existing. They are on us to advertise what we wear them to conceal.

In all ages, three-fourths of the support of the great charities has been conscience money.

There are no people who are quite so vulgar as the over-refined.

Be careless in your dress if you will but keep a tidy soul.

When you cannot get a compliment any other way, pay yourself one.

The main difference between a cat and a lie is that a cat only has nine lives.

History is strewn thick with evidence that a truth is not hard to kill, but a lie, well told, is immortal.

Truth is the most valuable thing we have. Let us economize it.

No real gentleman will tell the naked truth in the presence of ladies.

You should never do anything wicked and lay it on your brother, when it is just as convenient to lay it on some other boy.

The highest perfection of politeness is only a beautiful edifice, built, from the base to the dome, of ungraceful and gilded forms of charitable and unselfish lying.

Denial ain't just a river in Egypt.

We do not deal much in facts when we are contemplating ourselves.

A sin takes on a new and real terror when there seems a chance that it is going to be found out.

RELIGION

We despise all reverences and objects of reverence which are outside the pale of our list of sacred things and yet, with strange inconsistency, we are shocked when other people despise and defile the things which are holy for us.

Sacred cows make the best hamburger.

All saints can do miracles, but few of them can keep a hotel.

When I reflect upon the number of disagreeable people who I know who have gone to a better world, I am moved to lead a different life.

No sinner is ever saved after the first twenty minutes of the sermon.

We may not pay Satan reverence, for that would be indiscreet, but we can respect his talent.

God's great joke on the human race was requiring that men and women live together in marriage.

Nothing so needs reforming as other people's habits.

The dog is a gentleman; I hope to go to his heaven, not man's. Spirit has fifty times the strength and staying power of brawn and muscle.

Half the results of good intentions are evil; half the results of evil intentions are good.

It ain't those parts of the Bible that I can't understand that bother me, it is the parts that I do understand.

One mustn't criticize other people on grounds where he can't stand perpendicular himself.

When a man arrives at great prosperity God did it; when he falls into disaster he did it himself.

Providence protects children and idiots. I know because I have tested it.

A solemn, unsmiling, sanctimonious old iceberg who looked like he was waiting for a vacancy in the Trinity.

It is not best that we use our morals week days; it gets them out of repair for Sundays.

There is a charm about the forbidden that makes it unspeakably desirable.

There has only been one Christian. They caught and crucified him early.

Laws are sand, customs are rock. Laws can be evaded and punishment escaped, but an openly transgressed custom brings sure punishment.

I don't like to commit myself about heaven and hell—You see, I have friends in both places.

We have not the reverent feeling for the rainbow that a savage has, because we know how it is made. We have lost as much as we gained by prying into that matter.

The Bible is a mass of fables and traditions, mere mythology.

The more things are forbidden, the more popular they become.

The church is always trying to get other people to reform; it might not be a bad idea to reform itself a little, by way of example.

If Christ were here now there is one thing he would not be—a Christian.

The lack of money is the root of all evil.

There was never a century or a country that was short of experts who knew the Deity's mind and were willing to reveal it.

Nature knows no indecencies; man invents them.

Martyrdom covers a multitude of sins.

Heaven goes by favor; if it went by merit, you would stay out and your dog would go in.

If it is a miracle, any sort of evidence will answer, but if it is a fact, proof is necessary.

God, so atrocious in the Old Testament, so attractive in the New—the Jekyll and Hyde of sacred romance.

If there is a God, he is a malign thug.

Everything human is pathetic. The secret source of humor itself is not joy but sorrow. There is no humor in heaven.

To create man was a quaint and original idea, but to add the sheep was tautology.

He was a preacher, too . . . and he never charged nothing for his preaching, and it was worth it, too.

It is a good and gentle religion, but inconvenient.

Christianity will doubtless still survive in the earth ten centuries hence—stuffed and in a museum.

True irreverence is disrespect for another man's god.

(on Cain) It was his misfortune to live in a dark age that knew not the beneficent Insanity Plea.

The are many scapegoats for our sins, but the most popular is providence.

It is curious—curious that physical courage should be so common in the world, and moral courage so rare.

One of the proofs of the immortality of the soul is that myriads have believed it—they also believed the world was flat.

I believe our heavenly father invented man because he was disappointed in the monkey.

The universal brotherhood of man is our most precious possession, what there is of it.

The convention miscalled 'modesty' has no standard and cannot have one, because it is opposed to nature and reason and is therefore an artificiality and subject to anybody's whim—anybody's diseased caprice.

It is a blessed thing to have an imagination that can always make you satisfied, no matter how you are fixed.

Forget and forgive. This is not difficult when properly understood. It means forget inconvenient duties, then forgive yourself for forgetting. By rigid practice and stern determination, it comes easy.

It is agreed, in this country, that if a man can arrange his religion so that it perfectly satisfies his conscience, it is not incumbent on him to care whether the arrangement is satisfactory to anyone else or not.

An ethical man is a Christian—holding four aces.

Yet it was the schoolboy who said, "Faith is believing what you know ain't so."

Religion consists of a set of things which the average man thinks he believes and wishes he was certain.

But who prays for Satan? Who, in eighteen centuries, has had the common humanity to pray for the one sinner that needed it most?

What a man misses mostly in heaven is company.

(on the Bible) I have studied it often, but I could never discover the plot.

O lord our God, help us to tear their soldier to bloody shreds with our shells; help us to cover their smiling fields with the pale forms of their patriot dead; help us to drown the thunder of the guns with the shrieks of their wounded, writhing in pain; help us to lay waste their humble homes with a hurricane of fire; help us to wring the hearts of their unoffending widows with unavailing grief . . . for our sakes who adore Thee, Lord, blast their hopes, blight their lives, protract their bitter pilgrimage, make heavy their steps, water their way with their tears, stain the white snow with the blood of their wounded feet! We ask it in the spirit of love, of Him Who is the Source of Love, and Who is the ever faithful refuge and friend of all that are sore beset and seek His aid with humble and contrite hearts. Amen.

All right, then, I'll go to hell.

VICES AND VIRTUES

I haven't a particle of confidence in a man who has no redeeming vices.

Always acknowledge a fault. This will throw those in authority off their guard and give you an opportunity to commit more.

Temperance is best; intemperate temperance injures the cause of temperance.

Barring that natural expression of villainy which we all have, the man looked honest enough.

We can't reach old age by another man's road. My habits protect my life but they would assassinate you.

Good breeding consists of concealing how much we think of ourselves and how little we think of the other person.

Laws control the lesser man. Right conduct controls the greater one.

It is better to take what does not belong to you than to let it lie around neglected.

None of us can have as many virtues as the fountain pen, or half its cussedness; but we can try.

Except a creature be part coward, it is not a compliment to say he is brave.

It has always been my rule never to smoke when asleep, and never to refrain when awake.

To promise not to do a thing is the surest way in the world to make a body want to go and do that very thing.

Too much of anything is bad, but too much good whiskey is barely enough.

A human being has a natural desire to have more of a good thing than he needs.

Taking the pledge will not make bad liquor good, but it will improve it.

Some of us cannot be optimists, but all of us can be bigamists.

The man who is ostentatious of his modesty is twin to the statue that wears a fig-leaf.

I have made it a rule never to smoke more than one cigar at a time.

Some of his words were not Sunday-school words.

There ought to be a room in every house to swear in.

Few things are harder to put up with than the annoyance of a good example. Every time I reform in one direction I go overboard in another.

I deal with temptation by yielding to it.

Let us swear while we may, for in heaven it will not be allowed.

If I cannot smoke cigars in heaven, I shall not go.

The true pioneer of civilization is not the newspaper, not religion, not the railroad—but whiskey!

Any so-called material thing that you want is merely a symbol: you want it not for itself, but because it will content your spirit for the moment.

All the modern inconveniences.

In certain trying circumstances, urgent circumstances, desperate circumstances, profanity furnishes a relief denied even to prayer.

I make it a rule never to smoke while sleeping.

Water, taken in moderation, cannot hurt anybody.

Prosperity is the surest breeder of insolence I know.

Let us not be too particular; it is better to have old secondhand diamonds than none at all.

Sometimes too much to drink is barely enough.

New Year's Day—Now is the accepted time to make your regular annual good resolution. Next week you can begin paving hell with them as usual.

When angry, count to four; when very angry, swear.

The idea that a gentleman never swears is all wrong. He can swear and still be a gentleman if he does it in a nice and benevolent and affectionate way.

TRAVEL

Nothing so liberalizes a man and expands the kindly instincts that nature put in him as travel and contact with many kinds of people.

It is hopeless for the occasional visitor to keep up with Chicago—she outgrows his prophecies faster than he can make them up. She is always a novelty; for she is never the Chicago you saw when you last passed through.

Go to Heaven for the climate, Hell for the company.

France had neither winter nor summer nor morals—apart from these drawbacks it is a fine country.

When it's steamboat time, you steam.

I can understand German as well as the maniac that invented it, but I talk it best through an interpreter.

They spell it Vinci and pronounce it Vinchy; foreigners always spell better than they pronounce.

It used to be a good hotel, but that proves nothing—I used to be a good boy.

The educated Southerner has no use for l, and r, except at the beginning of a word.

All scenery in California requires distance to give it its highest charm.

The creator made Italy from designs by Michael Angelo.

I'm glad I did it, partly because it was worth it, but mostly because I shall never have to do it again.

There is a sumptuous variety about the New England weather that compels the stranger's admiration—and regret.

I have traveled more than any one else, and I have noticed that even the angels speak English with an accent.

In the South the war is what AD is elsewhere; they date from it.

If there is one thing that will make a man peculiarly and insufferably self-conceited, it is to have his stomach behave itself, on the first day at sea, when nearly all his comrades are seasick.

Climate is what we expect, weather is what we get.

I can speak French but I can't understand it.

The existing phrasebooks are inadequate. They are well enough as far as they go, but when you fall down and skin your leg they don't tell you what to say.

Only strangers eat tamarinds—but they only eat them once.

The people stared at us everywhere, and we stared at them. We bore down on them with America's greatness until we crushed them.

People born to be hanged are safer in water.

The gentle reader will never, never know what a consummate ass he can become until he goes abroad.

Distance lends enchantment to the view.

The coldest winter I ever spent was a summer in San Francisco.

In Boston they ask, how much does he know? In New York, how much is he worth? In Philadelphia, who were his parents.

Whenever the literary German dives into a sentence, that is the last you will see of him until he emerges on the other side of his Atlantic with his verb in his mouth.

There is probably no pleasure equal to the pleasure of climbing a dangerous Alp; but it is a pleasure which is confined strictly to people who can find pleasure in it.

The true charm of pedestrianism does not lie in the walking, or in the scenery, but in the talking. The walking is good to time the movement of the tongue by, and to keep the blood and the brain stirred up and active.

Travel is fatal to prejudice, bigotry, and narrow-mindedness.

I have found out there ain't no surer way to find out whether you like people or hate them than to travel with them.

Seasickness: at first you are so sick you are afraid you will die, and then you are so sick you are afraid you won't die.

Travel has no longer any charm for me. I have seen all the foreign countries I wish to see, except for heaven and hell, and I have only a vague curiosity as concerns one of those.

Cold! If the thermometer had been an inch longer we'd have frozen to death.

WORK

I do not like work, even when someone else does it.

Never put off till tomorrow what you can do the day after tomorrow.

He has been a doctor a year now and has had two patients, no, three, I think—yes, it was three; I attended their funerals.

Perseverance is a principle that should be commendable in those who have the judgment to govern it.

Man's mind clumsily and tediously patches little trivialities together and gets a result—such as it is.

To succeed in life, you need two things: ignorance and confidence.

Work consists of whatever a body is obligated to do . . . play consists of whatever a body is not obligated to do.

It usually takes more than three weeks to prepare a good impromptu speech.

The secret of getting ahead is getting started.

Obscurity and competence—that is the life that is best worth living.

There is nothing that saps one's confidence as the knowing how to do a thing.

There's always something about your success that displeases even your best friends.

Work is a necessary evil to be avoided.

What work I have done I have done because it was play. If it had been work I shouldn't have done it.

To succeed in other trades, capacity must be shown; in the law, concealment of it will do.

To be busy is a man's only happiness.

Anybody can write the first line of a poem, but it is a very difficult task to make the second line rhyme with the first.

Wine is a clog to the pen, not an inspiration.

Let us be thankful for the fools. But for them the rest of us could not succeed.

It is better to deserve honors and not have them than to have them and not deserve them.

Honest poverty is a gem that even a king might be proud to call his own—but I wish to sell out.

A crank is someone with a new idea—until it catches on.

Diligence is a good thing, but taking things easy is much more restful.

The less a man knows the bigger the noise he makes and the higher the salary he commands.

When a person cannot deceive himself the chances are against his being able to deceive other people.

A healthy and wholesome cheerfulness is not necessarily impossible to any occupation.

He is now rising from affluence to poverty.

Let's save the tomorrows for work.

MANKIND

Clothes make the man. Naked people have little or no influence on society.

Adam was the luckiest man; he had no mother-in-law.

Concerning differences between man and jackass: some observers hold there isn't any. But this wrongs the jackass.

Why was the human race created? Or at least why wasn't something creditable created in place of it? God had His opportunity. He could have made a reputation. But no, He must commit this gross folly—a lark which must have cost

Him a regret or two when he came to think it over and observe the effects.

The partitions of the houses were so thin we could hear the women occupants of adjoining rooms changing their minds.

The human race was always interesting and we know by its past that it will always continue so, monotonously.

Often it seems a pity that Noah and his party did not miss the boat.

Laughter without a tinge of philosophy is but a sneeze of humor. Genuine humor is replete with wisdom.

Man was made at the end of the week's work, when God was tired.

Humor is the great thing, the saving thing. The minute it crops up, all our irritation and resentments slip away, and the sunny spirit takes their place.

She was not quite what you would call refined. She was not quite what you would call unrefined. She was the kind of person who keeps a parrot.

When people do not respect us we are sharply offended; yet in his private heart no man much respects himself.

Apparently there is nothing that cannot happen today.

There's a good spot tucked away somewhere in everybody. You'll be a long time finding it, sometimes.

Children have but little charity for another's defects.

Thousands of geniuses live and die undiscovered—either by themselves or by others.

Everybody's private motto: It's better to be popular than right.

If man could be crossed with a cat, it would improve the man but deteriorate the cat.

The human race has only one really effective weapon and that is laughter.

Civilization is a limitless multiplication of unnecessary necessities.

Human beings feel dishonor the most, sometimes, when they most deserve it.

Let us consider that we are all partially insane. It will explain us to each other; it will unriddle many riddles; it will make clear and simple many things which are involved in haunting and harassing difficulties and obscurities now.

There is something fascinating about science. One gets such wholesale returns of conjecture out of such a trifling investment of fact.

Of all the animals, man is the only one that is cruel. He is the only one that inflicts pain for the pleasure of doing it.

They do not think at all; they only think they think.

Man is the only creature who has a nasty mind.

There are times when one would like to hang the whole human race, and finish the farce.

To eat is human, to digest, divine. Man is the only animal that blushes, or needs to.

To believe yourself brave is to be brave; it is the one essential thing.

We are all beggars, each in his own way.

Wit is the sudden marriage of ideas which before their union were not perceived to have any relation.

Man is the master of the unspoken word, which spoke, is master of him. All of us contain Music and Truth, but most of us can't get it out.

Fame is a vapor, popularity an accident; the only earthly certainty is oblivion.

We often feel sad in the presence of music without words; and often more than that in the presence of music without music.

A man's character may be learned from the adjectives which he habitually uses in conversation.

Human pride is not worthwhile; there is always something lying in wait to take the wind out of it.

If you pick up a starving dog and make him prosperous, he will not bite you.

That is the difference between dog and man.

He does not care for flowers. Calls them rubbish, and cannot tell one from another, and thinks it is superior to feel like that.

The human race is a race of cowards; and I am not only marching in that procession but carrying a banner.

It's good sportsmanship not to pick up lost balls while they are still rolling.

The man who does not read good books has no advantage over the man who cannot read them.

If man had created man he would have been ashamed of his performance.

Pity is for the living, envy is for the dead.

Circumstances make the man, not man the circumstances.

But when the time comes that a man has had his dinner, then the true man comes to the surface.

Good friends, good books and a sleepy conscience: this is the ideal life.

I am quite sure now that often, very often, in matters concerning religion and politics, a man's reasoning powers are not above the monkey's.

Laughter is the greatest weapon we have and we, as humans, use it least.

MISCELLANEOUS ADVICE

October. This is one of the peculiarly dangerous months to speculate in stocks. The others are July, January, September, April, November, May, March, June, December, August, and February.

It is better to keep your mouth closed and let people think you are a fool than to open it and remove all doubt.

If you hold a cat by the tail you learn things you cannot learn any other way.

Write without pay until someone offers to pay.

A man cannot be comfortable without his own approval.

Don't say the old lady screamed. Bring her on and let her scream.

Therein lies the defect of revenge: it's all in the anticipation; the thing itself is a pain, not a pleasure.

A successful book is not made of what is in it, but what is left out if it.

It may be called the master passion, the hunger for self-approval.

Words in haste do friendships waste.

Shut the door, not that it lets in the cold, but that it lets out the coziness.

A banker is a fellow who lends you his umbrella when the sun is shining and wants it back the minute it begins to rain.

A big leather-bound volume makes an ideal razor strap. A thin book is useful to stick under a table with a broken caster to steady it. A large, flat atlas can be used to cover a window with a broken pane. And a thick, old-fashioned heavy book with a clasp is the finest thing in the world to throw at a noisy cat.

It's not the size of the dog in the fight, it's the fight in the dog.

Buy land, they're not making it anymore.

There is nothing so annoying as to have two people talking when you're busy interrupting.

Have a place for everything, and keep the thing somewhere else.

Courage is resistance to fear, mastery of fear—not absence of fear.

The critic's symbol should be the tumble-bug: he deposits his egg in somebody else's dung, otherwise he could not hatch it.

I wonder how much it would take to buy a soap bubble, if there were only one in the world?

Be respectful of your superiors, if you have any.

The kernel, the soul—let us go further and say the substance, the bulk, the actual and valuable material of all human utterances—is plagiarism.

Do the thing you fear most and the death of fear is certain.

Name the greatest of all inventors. Accident.

A thing long expected takes the form of the unexpected when at last it comes.

Necessity is the mother of "taking chances."

(on the music of Wagner) Not as bad as it sounds.

It's easier to stay out than get out.

I like a story well told. That is the reason I am sometimes forced to tell them myself.

Necessity knows no law.

Nothing seems to please a fly so much as to be taken for a currant, and if it can be baked in a cake and palmed off on the unwary, it dies happy.

The wit knows that his place is at the tail end of a procession.

A man with a hump-backed uncle mustn't make fun of another man's cross-eyed aunt.

Books are for people who wish they were somewhere else.

If a person offends you, and you are in doubt as to whether it was intentional or not, do not resort to extreme measures; simply watch your chance and hit him with a brick.

There is a good side and a bad side to most people, and in accordance with your own character and disposition you will bring out one of them and the other will remain a sealed book to you.

Action speaks louder than words but not nearly as often.

When your watch gets out of order you have a choice of two things to do: throw it in the fire or take it to the watch tinker. The former is the quickest.

Part of the secret of success in life is to eat what you like and let the food fight it out inside.

It is wiser to find out than to suppose.

The calamity that comes is never the one we had prepared ourselves for.

If animals could speak, the dog would be a blundering outspoken fellow; but the cat would have the rare grace of never saying a word too much.

Let us endeavor to so live that when we come to die even the undertaker will be sorry.

All generalizations are false, including this one.

Be good and you will be lonely.

The weakest of all weak things is a virtue that has not been tested in the fire.

When red-haired people are above a certain social grade their hair is auburn.

Against the assault of laughter nothing can stand.

The proper office of a friend is to side with you when you are wrong.

His money is tainted: 'taint yours and 'taint mine.

A genuine expert can always foretell a thing that is 500 years away easier than he can a thing that's only 500 seconds off.

It is best to read the weather forecast before praying for rain.

Reputation is a hall-mark: it can remove doubt from pure silver, and it can also make the plated article pass for pure.

If you think knowledge is dangerous, try ignorance.

Be careful about reading health books. You might die of a misprint.

The cat, having sat upon a hot stove lid, will not sit upon a hot stove lid again. But he won't sit on a cold stove lid, either.

Golf is a good walk—spoiled.

The right word may be effective, but no word was ever as effective as a rightly timed pause.

There isn't a Parallel of Latitude but thinks it would have been an Equator if it had its rights.

Many a small thing has been made large by the right kind of advertising.

A dozen direct censures are easier to hear than one moronic compliment.

Humor is tragedy plus time.

A classic is something that everybody wants to have read and nobody wants to read.

It is a mistake that there is no bath that will cure people's manners, but drowning would help.

It is not best that we all should think alike, it is differences of opinion that make horse races.

Habit is . . . not to be flung out the window by any man, but coaxed downstairs a step at a time.

HIMSELF

I was born modest, but it wore off.

My books are water; those of the great geniuses are wine. Everybody drinks water.

I was seldom able to see an opportunity until it had ceased to be one.

I never take any exercise except sleeping and resting.

I respect a man who knows how to spell a word more than one way.

I can teach anybody how to get what they want out of life. The problem is that I can't find anybody who can tell me what they want.

Repartee is something we think of twenty-four hours too late.

I am a border ruffian from the State of Missouri, I am a Connecticut Yankee by adoption, In me you have Missouri morals, Connecticut culture; this gentlemen, is the combination which makes the perfect man.

I am prepared to meet anyone, but whether anyone is prepared for the great ordeal of meeting me is another matter.

I thoroughly believe that any man who's got anything worthwhile to say will be heard if he only says it often enough.

I was gratified to be able to answer promptly. I said, "I don't know."

There has been much tragedy in my life: at least half of it actually happened.

I, Mark Twain being of sound mind, have spent everything.

The Public is merely a multiplied "me."

I was sorry to have my name mentioned among the great authors because they have a sad habit of dying off.

I would much rather have my ignorance than another man's knowledge, because I have so much of it.

I know all those people. I have friendly, social, and criminal relations with the whole lot of them.

I could have become a soldier if I had waited; I knew more about retreating than the man who invented retreating.

I am not the editor of a newspaper and shall always try to do right and be good so that God will not make me one.

Thrusting my nose firmly between his teeth, I threw him heavily to the ground on top of me.

I cannot keep from talking, even at the risk of being instructive.

I didn't attend the funeral, but I sent a nice letter saying I approved of it.

I have been an author for 22 years and an ass for 55.

It takes me a long time to lose my temper, but once lost, I could not find it with a dog.

The rain is famous for falling on the just and unjust alike, but if I had the management of such affairs I would rain softly and sweetly on the just, but if I caught a sample of the unjust out doors I would drown him.

I am opposed to millionaires, but it would be dangerous to offer me the position.

There is nothing you can answer to a compliment. I have been complimented myself a great many times and they always embarrass me—I always feel they haven't said enough.

He had only one vanity; he thought he could give advice better than any other person.

I could have made a neat retort but didn't, for I was flurried and didn't think of it till I was downstairs.

I am losing enough sleep to supply a worn-out army.

I would much prefer to suffer from the clean incision of an honest lancet than from a sweetened poison.

I thoroughly disapprove of duels. If a man should challenge me, I would take him kindly and forgivingly by the hand and lead him to a quiet place and kill him.

Quitting smoking is easy. I've done it a thousand times.

He was as shy as a newspaper is when referring to his own merits.

I must have a prodigious quantity of mind: it takes me as much as a week sometimes to make it up.

I was born excited.

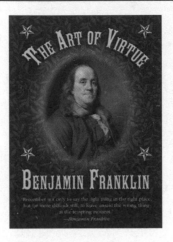

The Art of Virtue

Ben Franklin's Formula for Successful Living

Benjamin Franklin

Benjamin Franklin once wrote that he had "conceived the bold and arduous project of arriving at moral perfection . . . [and] wished to live without committing any fault at any time . . . to conquer all that either natural inclination, custom, or company might lead me into." Although he was never able to finish this project completely, Benjamin Franklin was able to lay down the beginnings of this work in his later writings. Collected here for the first time are essays by Benjamin Franklin on living a virtuous life. Starting with Franklin's essay "Art of Virtue," read on to find out his thoughts on justice, moderation, chastity, and more.

This is an easy-to-read guide to living your life with as much virtue as possible, the way Benjamin Franklin envisioned it could be.

$9.95 Hardcover • ISBN 978-1-61608-331-1

ALSO AVAILABLE

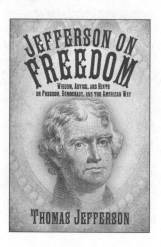

Jefferson on Freedom

Wisdom, Advice, and Hints on Freedom, Democracy, and the American Way

Thomas Jefferson

Thomas Jefferson is most famous for the writing of the Declaration of Independence, which espouses the general principles of freedom and democracies that Americans hold dear. Now, collected here for the first time, is this historical American document, as well as several of his other famous writings. Included in this book are excerpts from his only full-length book, *Notes on the State of Virginia*, letters to Samual Kercheval and Edward Carrington on liberal democracy and freedom, and an exchange with Danbury Baptists regarding the right to religious freedom. Jefferson provides excellent and timeless quotes on attaining freedom and living a democratic life.

$9.95 Hardcover • ISBN 978-1-61608-289-5

ALSO AVAILABLE

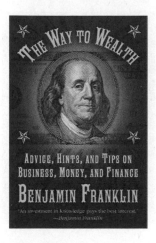

The Way to Wealth

Advice, Hints, and Tips on Business, Money, and Finance

Benjamin Franklin

Ben Franklin's writings have inspired millions throughout the years, and his advice on how to earn and save money is timeless. *The Way to Wealth* is a collection of Franklin's essays and personal letters on how to make money, start a business, and save for the future. Essays include "Advice to a Young Tradesman," which explains how to run a profitable business; "The Whistle," a charming parable on how to prevent greed from trumping profitability; and "On Smuggling, and its Various Species," which reveals the reasons cheaters never succeed. All will help and inspire you on your glorious way to wealth and prosperity.

Also included is Franklin's "The Way to Make Money Plenty in Every Man's Pocket," tidbits from *Poor Richard's Almanack*, personal letters to his sister chock-full of advice for a prosperous household, and more! In tough economic times, this book is for anyone who longs for financial stability and growth.

$9.95 Hardcover • ISBN 978-1-61608-201-7

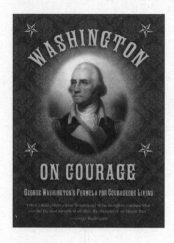

Washington on Courage

George Washington's Formula for Courageous Living

George Washington

George Washington was the senior officer of the colonial forces during the first stages of the French and Indian War, the commander in chief of the Continental Army during the American Revolution, the man who presided over the Constitutional Convention that drafted the United States Constitution, and the first president of what became the United States of America; is it any wonder we look to this brave and forward-thinking man for inspiration on how to live with courage and honor? Including letters to friends and foes during the French and Indian War and the American Revolution, orders and instructions to the troops, and speeches he gave during his life, collected here are essays and advice by George Washington on living a courageous life.

$9.95 Hardcover • ISBN 978-1-61608-703-6